FORGET ME NOT

Poetry by

Peter I. Webster

Grosvenor House
Publishing Limited

This book is published by
Grosvenor House Publishing Ltd
Link House
140 The Broadway, Tolworth, Surrey, KT6 7HT.
www.grosvenorhousepublishing.co.uk

A CIP record for this book
is available from the British Library

ISBN 978-1-83615-210-1

To Christine.

INTRODUCTION

This book is, in part, dedicated to those affected directly
or indirectly by Dementia, be it as a carer or through
the relationship of a loved one.
It is a shadow cast on so many lives and
unfortunately this shadow does not disappear with the
setting of the sun.
Keep the bond you have with family and grow
positively through the experience.
Like so many challenges in life it shall be overcome
eventually.

The poems in Forget Me Not vary widely in topic,
but reference is also made to COVID with a mix of
humour shed on a very unhappy period for many.
Gone but not forgotten it touched everyone, but has not
been laid to rest, this pestilence a disease, a pest,
another test of which there are seemingly many.
We can reminisce, but heed we must and leave the cure to
those we trust.
The cause unnecessary in many ways will haunt generations
for millions of days into the future, but fight we must.
Follow the strength of the people now passed this is not
the world's first challenge and will not be our last.

CONTENTS

SLIPPING AWAY

Sometimes I feel you're slipping
Slip, slip, slipping away.
Sometimes I feel you're slipping
But you come back the very next day.

Slip stream is how I see it
A force pulling you away,
But you sometimes use the slip stream
To return the very next day.

In and out of the slip stream
Like a car on the racing track,
You use the force of the slip stream
And the next day you're here, you are back.

My greatest fear each day
Is that we are running out of track
The slip stream is disappearing
And may never bring you back.

I say a prayer for the slip stream
I pray it will always be there
As it brings you back momentarily
In the way that you always were.

ADVICE

When I give advice, it is a gift
To help in troubled times and ease the rift.
Do you hear my words
Do you think they are absurd?

Troublesome people are everywhere
Making difficult situations
For those who really care.
Wretched so and heading for disaster.
Though they don't know.

Do you see me as a friend
When those matters you once dealt with ease
Now seem hard to mend?
The message or suggestions are to help,
They are all well intended that I send.

THE BIG 'A' IS HERE

I refuse to blame myself because the big A is here.
I'd rather laugh it off or drink a pint of beer.
No I'm not coming down with it; at least I don't think so?
It's just that I am noticing it more clearly as I grow.

I remember my old Uncle Ned who had imaginary friends
    and family; they would simply laugh and refer to it as a
    senior moment, just around the bend.

Oh yes they'd take it seriously of course and help in many ways,
    but today is far different from those of my younger days.

And Grandma too, became afflicted at the age of eighty plus,
    my main concern being visualised when given the task to
    escort her home by bus!

Oh yes those were the days, when we took it in our stride, no
    magic pills or potions, no care homes in which to hide.
But the big A hits a serious note when it comes more close to
    home, the anger and the pain is mixed with loneliness
    and pride,
For there's no current cure, just true friends who will stay
    close by their side.

IT BEGINS WITH 'A'?

What is it I have acquired?
A fuzz, a mental block,
A mist which removes desire.
It crept upon me like a thief,
It stole into my space.
This thing, this melancholy sponge
Has robbed me of my grace.
What is it called? Begins with A…
The name reminds me of a war,
A camp, a prison of the mind,
Destroyed what my memory was for.
Why am I here, what have I done?
Why has my life become so glum?
It begins with 'A' … and reminds me of me.

LITTLE THINGS MATTER

It's the little things that matter
The cup of tea in the morning,
Before you have even stopped yawning,
The empty cereal bowl, in place
Ready and waiting to start the day
and help you on your busy way.

It's the little things that matter,
"After you" in a busy queue.
A helping arm across the street
And a smile on your face for strangers
You meet.

It's the little things that matter
Your pride before a fall,
The acceptance of a loss,
The refusal to get cross.

It's the little things that matter
Which is much harder than you think.
Just take a look at your day gone by
Then answer truly, squarely eye to eye
No fingers crossed or cheeky wink.

MEET ME AT THE GATE

Though it is getting late and we shall never know our fate,
All I ask of you my friend is meet me at the gate.
The gate has two sides, two sides to realise.
Always leave it open, never use the lock
And when you're feeling lonely, just feel it sway and rock.
Soak up all that life has for you, all that's on your plate,
Never fear I'll be there for you when you meet me at the gate.

NO GOOD TO ARGUE

Arguing is tough,
When your point of view is never heard
And the day's not long enough.

Arguing is hard,
As if we have been dealt the wrong card.
Do the words then cut like a shard of glass
And bleed inside until the moments pass?

Arguing is cruel,
Like a vicious duel
That makes life sad and lame,
Causing doubt and pain
Without sensitivity or gain.

Arguing is unfulfilling
As worthless as the King's Shilling.
A war on words for ones differing ideals
Buried like time in an open field.

REVERSE ENGINEERING

This is a question for the body and the mind.
How can I rebuild myself using principles of this kind?
Take the knowledge you have gained in moving through
    life's field, strip it back from where you are, use
    experience like a shield.
Build it back, avoiding those pitfalls that you've found,
Fill them in with safety, logic and common sense,
Not there the first time round.
Practice and re engineer at the end of every day
Rebuild your life, your world's environment, your dreams,
make the journey easier that way.

FAT CAT AMBITION

There is a time and there is a place,
You are always there to fill a space,
Sometimes needed sometimes not,
Sometimes remembered, sometimes forgot.

The time the place on earth, the space
Where and when depends on your own pace,
Depends on the reason, the choices we make,
Depends on your conscience and those we forsake.

Around every corner lies the unknown,
Beyond each horizon we have not yet been shown,
But do your deed well with a conscience bright
Not with a heart as black as the night.

We all think we're right and we all do our best
We all put others to our own test,
But cruelty and cunning sadly reign supreme,
With the ladder of ambition and self esteem.

Pay attention and look, for the further you climb
The rungs disappear and become a fine line.
They won't always be there to handle your weight
And for fat cat ambition, support comes too late.

LESSON FROM A TREE

Trees don't go on holiday
They simply change day by day,
No movement visible to the naked eye
As they reach majestically for the sky.

No trees stay firmly planted
Held fast by strong and searching roots
Which grow their full height and more
To feed from earths rich and bountiful store.

Trees do their work, they never rest
All year round they do their best,
Providing shade and food and shelter as a host
They never lie or cheat or boast.

And their reward, if left by man
A healthy, carefree long life span.
And will outlast both you and me
Who fade more quickly than the tree.

LIFE'S MYSTERY

Life is our mystery from start to end,
We, only we, can comprehend.
I have heard it said, enjoy the day, we never know what lies
    ahead.

Wise words yet easier said than done,
As the plan though good might be tripped,
Detached, undone.

Yet if we should know what lies ahead,
There would be times when we might turn and stay in bed.
Fear of looking beyond the door,
In denial of what life has in store.

That's our mystery which we search each day
The knowing not, the future bright or in disarray.

Planning and dreaming are never appearing,
It's action we need to allow.
No use pretending that life's never ending
Just make your life good here and now.

CHRISTMAS IN LOCKDOWN

An empty house, soulless gloom, solitude in an empty room.
Christmas on your own is like Sunday with tinsel or a letter
    written to yourself in pencil?
No church congregation,
No cause for pause or elation.
Christmas alone is not one for celebration.

Christmas alone gives time to reflect,
Time to remember the things we neglect.
Christmas in solitude is no Christmas at all,
For some it's more TV or simply staring at the wall!
But for some, we can learn the meaning of patience,
Give thought to what others might say?
Rather than preaching your own views day after day.
I have learned quite a lot from this day home alone.
No extravagance, no rushinhg around, the pleasure of
    listening to the sound of no sound.
The pleasure of music which I might select,
Not listening to adverts, on which my life interject.
Christmas in solitude, it isn't that bad,
If you like your own company or that of one friend,
Then you've found the real reason for Christmas, after all, in
    the end.

BROTHERS

May your differences be small ones
May you always know how to forgive
Leave time to enjoy and live.
Don't allow a grudge the space in your life
Reserved for tranquility.
Don't make a burden cast upon you a liability
Know yourself and your brother
Always make time for one another.

WHAT IF?

What if I had a million Pounds?
What if all dreams could be bought?
Ones own dreams would be worthless
And ones efforts count for naught.

What if a man was penniless?
What if each dream he earned?
I could talk to him in confidence
And be richer for the lessons learned.

ONCE NEW

The old bicycle rests against the wall
And no one cares if it should fall
Its wheels are rusty, chain and brakes too
Hard to imagine it once was new.

The old sofa lies on the rubbish tip
Its covers in tatters, the seams about to rip
And from the cushions a spring peeps through
Hard to imagine it once was new.

The old car stands in the breakers yard
The wheels are gone, the body looks cold and hard,
The colours now dull once were a shining blue
Hard to imagine it once was new.

The old man stares into the crowd
His eyes now dim begin to cloud
Tired and weak his past thoughts review
Hard to imagine he once was new.

VICTORIAN VALUES

Long passed, long gone
The pride upheld, now is there none?
It is a privilege I now feel
To have witnessed that Victorian zeal.
A sense of making a lot,
From what little they had got.
Never spend a penny when a ha' penny
would do,
Make do and mend that old, worn out shoe!
Never hang your dirty washing on the line,
Always keep your watch set just ahead of time.
Stomach in and chest out, though there may be little to
    shout about.
The stiff upper lip exchanged for a pout.

Yes I'm privileged to have witnessed this,
The strong hand shake replaced by a kiss,
Meaning little or naught, but one moment
caught.
It's not to say it was better that way
Though complaining meant little in Victoria's day.

Grandad was born in 1876, great uncles and aunts born at
    this time, led by example
not given to whine.
Make do and mend, a life of simplicity,
Don't boast, keep to your modesty
Like the never bending old oak tree.
It's hard to imagine that in this day,
When everyone want their feelings
hung out on display.
So what is the difference between now and then?
The now generation of borrow today and tomorrow, God
    send.
The now generation of, just bail me out,
The champagne crowd who may find it has all been replaced
    by a more modest bottle of stout.

MOVIE OF LIFE

It starts with that bundle which takes title role
An unwritten work, the story of a soul.
A flat screen, blank canvas
The star of a theme,
Which has not yet been written,
The start of a dream.
Act one, scene one, the chapter is set.
Will the movie be happy or one of regret?
You learn all the movements, the tumbles, the spills,
The can do's and can't, those impossible drills.
Laughter and comedy, crying at night
Amazement each day at the dawn's early light.
You take all the cues, the action, the cuts.
The highway before you with all those deep ruts.
Before you can walk, you must learn to crawl,
Soon you are steady and knowing it all.
But that is the intro, the theme is to come,
The rhymes and the reason, rhythm set to the beat of the
    drum.
The March of life's journey is on the way,
With only one twist, there'll be no rehearsal or chance to
    replay!

Each day's an adventure an unknown ordeal
Sometimes delightful and sometimes unreal.
Sometimes a test of you and the rest.
Where is your standing compared with the best?
The things which you like and those things you don't.
The choices you could make and those which you won't.
Which role shall you take, the villain, the star,
Director too?
This movie rolls on, all parts played by you.

THE PIT

And yet I miss it;
Never a beauty, rather a beast
A scruffy mix of shambles, rambles and undulating streets.
White scrubbed steps with concave mould
To greet the travellers who crossed this threshold.

Chimneys, black brick and tall, the people below; so small.
Smoke filled air left its blackened scar on everything they
    wear,
House proud people, mend, repair every rip or tear to hide
    the poverty and strip bare,
As if to camouflage what little they had
And paint a portrait of life, not grand, but not so bad.

It was never so long ago that men would march in unison
    down the same dank lane,
Towards a danker hole, with steel clad feet,
Clipping the cobbles with a military beat
And silence broken once with each acknowledgment and
    greet.

The shift that started with a hoot
and finished with bodies blackened by the dust and soot.
Skin pores saturated with the grime that remained
    stubbornly over time, to be forced forward only through
    the sweat
And stain their white starched collar blacker yet.

And yes I miss it;
Miss the song, the melody
That these souls conjured out in harmony.
The noise, the smokey bar, the fresh face
of a youth before entrapment into this place.

NEW NORMAL

New normal, what is this?
We have never had a normal
And I don't think such exists.
Yes we've had the routine
We've had the daily drudge,
But new normal never cut it
And my point of view won't budge.
These phrases are invented
By those without a clue,
Who think that our new normal
Refers to standing in a queue!
Wearing masks, a new fashion trend
What message is this supposed to send?
When walking around like faceless souls,
Eyes open wide or tightly shut
To understand what we are told
Through muffled voices behind a mask
What kind of new normal is this I ask?

DIAMOND IN THE ROUGH

You might say I'm rough around the edges
A diamond in the rough?
But I think I'm more a softer touch
Like satin, silk or a ball of fluff!

I'd like to set the diamond square
Into its rightful place, not just thin air.
To see it shine like claret wine,
And not simply hang upon an unripened Vine.

Oh yes; a diamond in the rough,
But are we crystal, not so tough?
Or shards of glass, a splintered frame
With nothing to border that forgotten name.

The carbonaceous rock upon which our standard's lie,
A monumental feast set into each human eye,
Which likened to an hypnotic trance
Might lead us on a Dervish dance
To spin and swirl in mysterious form
Back in time to the place we're born.

ARTIFICIAL INTELLIGENCE

Artificial intelligence
That is a lot to understand
Considering we haven't yet got to grips with
Human Intelligence, currently in hand!

A little knowledge is a dangerous thing
Intelligence per se does need more nurture and
    understanding
And understanding requires much more than
an artificial brain,
It takes humility, a lack of pride and undivided thought to
    remove the prejudice inside.

For prejudice blocks, transfers, our thoughtful colours to
    dullish blurs.
It reduces all to black and white
Which leads to our confusion,
The simplification to AI will not provide
conclusion.

WHERE WERE YOU?

Where were you
In sixty three or in eighty
Where were you when,
Kennedy and Lennon met their demise?
Why do we know
And do we feel sorrow?

Where were you in Forty Five
Those of us who are still alive.
Where were you in sixty eight
Or later still in Water Gate?
Those events which influence history
Surrounded in a novel of mystery.

The events of life, imprinted on minds
For whatever reason or human design.
History repeated, changes man made,
Through weapons of force, real or unseen
Shall affect life's reality and replace all of life's
dreams.

EXCUSING HINDSIGHT

It is the people, the people who go forward and carry on
While politicians ponder, procrastinate on what was done,
  In hindsight, wrong.
The time so wasted, sweep it away.
The people head down, let us get on with another day.

The legal eagles rub their hands as they profess their noble
  skills,
Cross questioning, provoking the errors made,
Like re reading a chapter from Marquis de Sade.
Excuses spill more freely than ink from a blunted quill
And the stories of hindsight fill up the legal's till.

What nonsense, what is done is done, despite what we have
  learned,
Those lessons will be forgotten and soon shall be returned.

FLOATING ON THIN AIR

I think it was a wake up call this year
Last year ended and I was not in top gear.
Oh yes; I have had my scares, my side swipes in life,
But nothing quite as debilitating as realising the fragility of
    life.
I have done quite well, so far,
At 72 with only the superficial battle scar;
The knee, the back, the leg that festered from a knock,
Now all healed and out of dock.
You could say I thought myself as solid as a rock!
But sometimes life has other plans
We find ourselves on shifting sands
That slip and slide from side to side,
Traction is hard, as is the ride.
But it's at this time, you need that upper lip.
The belief in the bigger picture, the will,
The thumb aloft and a white knuckle grip.
Yet the question will still be there.
Have I survived or am I floating on a cloud of thin air?

GOOD INTENTIONS

I must help those children with a cleft
Or those suffering with Trachoma,
those plights, those losing fights,
Those children left alone.

It is my good intention, every waking day,
To help the needy, cure the sick, remember when I pray.
Though good intention is not enough, they
simply appease our mind.
And suffering continues in all the alleyways of mankind.

I don't know how I should address a challenged individual,
Am I politically incorrect or expressing what is actual?
More accent upon correctness rather than the scourge,
Wake up and smell the coffee, good intentions
please, I urge.

Good intentions follow all our lives,
The streets are paved with these,
But charities set to help, start with their own needs and
    families
And what is left is given to every major cause,
From homelessness to hunger caused by good intentioned
    wars.

REALITY

It's so important to make acknowledgements in life,
None more important than to acknowledge what is called
   reality.
Society however appears obliged
To shield us all from this form of brutality.

We cannot play God, try as we might
To put hardships out of plain sight
Or cure all the sick, prevent working hard
In order we all avoid the red card.

No critics allowed,
Just keep your head bowed.
Whilst those chosen few are placed in spaces
And shown a debt of gratitude.
Don't disrupt is the new norm, to make correction is now
   rude.

FAITH

Trust in God
Whomsoever it may be
Trust and believe
Though your belief maybe a deity.

Trust in your God
As we are meant to do
Do not enforce your disbelief
On those less brave than you.

Do not enforce your own belief
For each one has their reason,
Allow time for your fellow man
They also have a Season

Be true to faith and you shall find
A better life shall call,
There's no need to fight to prove yourself
As God will find us all.

THE COVID IF

If we can start a task
And see it through to its completion
Whilst we stick to it without omission or deletion.
If we can isolate and hide
And not be in fear of hiding,
If we can create an impenetrable bubble
Yet refrain from getting in a huddle.
If we can queue and not be tired of queuing and keep a
    distance, don't get too close
Or stand alone for hours on end,
Then the virus will pass on by
While we, the public, rebuke the danger and treat each new
    measure as a necessary trend.
If we can pretend at ten p.m. that the virus is asleep.
Walk home, don't run, just creep
And before you go indoors take a peep.
If we can make sure that the coast is clear,
As we finish up our ten p.m. beer.
If we can wash our hands and face,
Before we enter any space
And be as clean as we can be,
Then the virus will leave both you and me
And we shall once again be free.

If we can learn to understand all that is politically grand
And do what we are ordered to
Until Covid has given up its ill intent
And the last germ is dead and spent.
If we can undo, in time, all that has been undone,
If we can make sense out of others nonsense and deliberation
    yet be responsible for our own salvation, until we have
    become one new nation.
If we can take each stolen Covid minute and replace it with
    a better one,
Then we can mark this great yet solemn occasion
And which is more we shall be our own man, once again,
    my son.

HOW TO WEAR A MASK

Is there no real news ?
As we are guided by mindless interviews.
Laymen of all kinds are given the task
To educate us all on how to wear a mask.
Don't hang it from your ear,
You'll simply look a little queer!
Don't have it underneath your nose,
The germ will see the route and up it goes!
Don't wear it underneath your chin,
You'll look a complete chump when you grin.
Simply wear it as a bank robber would,
For your own and everyone else's good.

ANSWER TO COVID

You didn't kill me off
You just laid me low,
It was the actions of insanity
Which dealt the killer blow.

I am pleased to say you missed
And left a wounded prey,
Which healed and mended slowly
Day by waking day.

You opened up my eyes
To the wrongs within our world
Which become an entangled theme
Mixed with the ambition of one's own
unreal dream.

But I'm pleased, I have recovered
And no longer hold a grudge,
I saw the light and understand
It is no ones place to judge.

A CHRISTMAS DAY

What would we say to A Christmas Day
With little on our plate?
What would we say to a day of gloom
Without a light to brighten up the room.
No warmth, no fire, no turkey feast,
No decorations on the tree,
Indeed no fun or frivolity.

What would we say if an infant child had not been born this
    day?
What would we say if the Magi had not passed his way?
Had left no mark of his arrival or presence.
What would we say?

There would be nothing to say or feel
Our being would have little support,
A void, a crevasse, a gaping hole
Nothing to link the spirit with the soul.
Though now we can hope, we can rejoice,
We have a link to what we are
To follow remains simply one of choice.

FIGHT THE GOOD FIGHT

We can fight our wars against guns and bombs.
We can stand against the enemy long after they are gone,
But give us pestilence and disease
And rationality of great minds appear to freeze.
Where has belief in greater powers than ours
disappeared to
Has belief replaced itself, discarded, alone and on the shelf?
We can sacrifice our sons and daughters,
Lead them all to mindless slaughter
And qualify all good reasons or quote a man for all our
    seasons.
Yet infect our bodies with poisoned air
And intelligence dims to become a blur.
Confusion reigns supreme and nightmares create themselves
    from a simple dream.

LOST TO BE FOUND

As I drifted from the shore
I lost my compass, I lost my oar.
Watching helpless as land disappeared
Visions of a future, which now I feared.

We all seek security, that fixed abode
A view or vision on an open road.
A vision of warmth is in my mind
A sheltered view comforting and kind.

Is this more than one should ask,
Is the aim a futile task?
For some I guess, the answer is yes,
For others a show of the power to impress.

Which side of the road that you are on
Depends on which road you are born,
For life is the challenge, nothing is free
It is all down to the efforts of you and of me.

Nothing prepares us for what we must face,
No hand outs, no free lunch, no blessing or grace.
Only your effort right from the start
Will decide if you're flying or falling apart.

There is no guarantee for what life has in store,
Just tranquil moments followed by tempests galore
And the refuge you'll find is in your state of mind,
Keep peace in your heart, be brave and be kind.

AHEAD OF TIME

Never let age move faster than you,
See the way, before Father Time
Can see the finish line.

Wish you'd done it differently?
Many people do,
But if you'd done it differently
Then, you would not be you.

Wish you were Mick Jagger,
Another Rolling Stone?
But if you were you'd gather no moss
And still be on your own.

Wish you were John Lennon or Nureyev in dance,
But if you were, life would be short
And peace won't stand a chance
Or Wish you were like Jesus
Another rising star?
But if you were like Jesus
You wouldn't get that far.

Simply be yourself in life
And swim through tide sometimes,
Until you reach the waters edge,
Eyes open, wiser, maybe blind.
Don't pander for a different life,
Just make it different, if you can.
Try your best and simply face, what exactly is life's short span.

STATE OR PRIVATE

Education, everyone deserves the same,
State or Private, but which system holds the blame.
We hold in high esteem our system which
Supports every dream.
Supports effort and supports affliction,
Supports our disadvantaged and supports addiction.
Yet more is never enough
And to criticise one is like dropping a bomb
On one student who tries regardless of state
Versus one student whose life is marred with
envy and adult infused hate.
The children of state, we are to believe, are lacking and
    needing who also need feeding.
While the privileged class of educative luxury are cocooned
    and need nothing, the rich toffs of life, but perhaps this
    short view ignores their own sacrifice.
Nothing comes easy, it's our youth which is framed on both
    sides of the fence, without being named, pulled and
    pushed regardless of need, while pointing the finger and
    watching two systems bleed.

TOO MANY CHIEFS

Is it a new trend for everyone to want the top job and no one
    wants the supporting role?
No one wants to take the pick and shovel,
But everyone wants to view the hole.
"I can do it better" is the chant we hear
Over cups of coffee or a glass of beer.

Who do they think they are?
On another swan.
Only just returned unpacked and packed,
Then again they're gone.
Who is running this or that?
They are rarely ever seen.
While I, am burning midnight oil
My eyes shaped like the screen.

I'm questioned till ideas spill,
Then mysteriously appear,
The one on top throws out my thoughts,
It is all their big idea.

Are we busy playing games
Or really doing stuff?
We know we're doing little,
But who will call our bluff?

To challenge, the on line shopping list,
The illness that is faked,
The turn to collect the kids from school,
Excuses all half baked.

Anything to make life's toil seem hard,
The pressures we all face.
Reality is there's very few can take the baton at full pace.
Perhaps we now have got the gist,
We can drop that "untrue" excuse list
And accept ambition is misplaced in most
Or that the best pretenders hold top post.

The Chess board has more pawns than Kings,
That's how the game is won.
It's the graft that builds from foundation up
which will support the dome.
Who wants to build, who sacrifices time?
These virtues which are missed,
Replaced by craft and scheming plans,
Short cuts to fill that gaping rift.

WHAT'S THE REASON?

Why are we here?
To live each day and face whatever
challenge may come our way
Or console ourselves with charity
As a Mass for those who choose to pay?

Should we believe in life itself
As a challenge set for us to face
Or envy those who are seemingly blessed
And placed on high in a far better place?

Are we ruled by the TV screen
And images in life we would never dare dream
Or do we choose to help fellow man
On routine levels without any plan?

The choice is yours think long and hard
No need to challenge ourselves on our own dealt card.
Take the day, as it comes your way
and bless all goodness,
Simple deeds over which you may purvey.

SPOILED SOCIETY

I am referring to all concerned
We are a population of an ever growing number of groups.
All of which expect recognition, box tick, but all want their
    own way, questionable box tick, impossible box tick?
Hey, take a break, take a pause, observe the rules and obey
    the laws.
We know, we hear the complaints and concerns aired and
    viewed, but what suits all is overly skewed.
Disruption to others is never the way when you block the
    roads or block someone's way.
We absorb what we can, in fact few do more,
But take an unselfish view, I implore.
Don't act like children or worse, disregard others rights to
    verse.
Don't stamp and cry or feel the world has passed you by.
Get on with your life, day by day and life will be made far
    better if you avoid getting in to each other's way.

WE HAVE LOWERED THE BAR FAR TOO FAR

Standards have disappeared as we have feared.
No pass, no fail
Do as you please and perhaps, no jail.

I don't want to sound melancholy, but if your only aim in
    life is the sky, fresh cream and apple pie,
Then you are going to come up very shy.

Our lives are challenged each and everyone
No preferential treatment, not for anyone.
It's a slog and the choices we make
Need to be right as there will be no retake.
Just another challenge to set yourself within.
So stand up, dust off and take it on the chin.

Take it on the chin, start again
The disappointment, second best and all the other pain.
Look ahead and then beyond life is more than a magic
    wand.
Though magic life can be if you choose to be cool and live in
    serenity.

MAKING-HAY

Life is tough,
Of that there's no doubt,
But that is what life is all about.
Strike for more pay if you must,
Just be careful whom you can trust.
Don't sacrifice low pay for no pay
Realise what happens when searching
for your, Making-hay day.

WHAT HAS GOD GOT
TO DO WITH IT?

What does God think of our madness?
The creator of life, the witness of such sadness.
Has life presented so much tragedy, since the dawn of time
Or has escalation become the norm,
Because it is available on line.
Whereas before no one knew what was happening right in
front of you.
No reports, no news, no acknowledgement ,
Just sadness for those close to the event.

TWO WRONGS

Disaster is approaching fast
At least that's what we hear.
A monumental, syncopated blast,
Looming catastrophe is crystal clear

Ice is melting as we speak, glaciers disappear,
The Ozone layer is no more, children filled with fear.
We care about the air we breath, removed from reality
Resplendent in our cushioned life, no thought of their
    mortality.

Starvation echoes everywhere, old as history or time.
The images which we advertise, but it's their concern not
    mine.
The plagues of our self righteousness and self inflicted
    wounds.
Contradictions from the wise might not correct
our doom.

Strangely though our planet also contributes
With natural disasters, its own air does pollute.
The answer, no one "truly" knows and solutions we can't
    find.
Until we've gone full circle with no one left behind?

Yes, our situation is serious,
We are all in a fix,
As we continue to shrink the countryside with
more tarmac roads and bricks.

The answer is that we're all wrong
Two wrongs never make it right,
Wisdom is as wisdom does to solve the planet's plight.
Einstein's theory takes us back in time
And other clever sums,
But perhaps there is some light to shed
For tomorrow never comes?

RETURN TO UK TO FEEL SICK

I've lived all my life in tropical climes
And never caught disease,
I have spent 40 years in the tropics
With not so much as a sneeze.

But returning to my home land
I wonder in dismay how sickness
Wells up throughout the year
From May to Christmas Day.

Is it for a day off work or just our social track,
Are we a sick society or all hypochondriacs?
There's every form of flu, hay fever in May too
And gastroenteritis, we are never off the loo.

We really are a poorly bunch,
I don't think we've always been that way.
It must be stress or leaking bits,
At least that's what the adverts say.

Now there! Blame it on the adverts
They tell us what we need,
The vitamins to cure ourselves
Before we go to seed.

HUNGER

We All need a reality check
I am white, so can't address
A point of view which might distress
Those, which society may oppress.
Best say nothing as more means less.
Just feed the hungry,
Where Ethnicity has no place
For Malnutrition does not depend
Upon the colour of your face.

MALAYSIAN ISLAND VIEW

I saw an Eagle glide across the sky one day
And then circled overhead by a secluded bay.
Two Orioles flew into the trees that overlooked the ocean
And sang their morning song with neither intention nor
    emotion.

The morning wakes to natures sound,
The birds break out in chorus
And nothing can their symmetry disturb
For they know they were here before us.

A sunbird wends its way with apparent indirection,
But once upon a flower's stem it suckles with perfection.
The clouds form in their wispy banks surreal in their
    splendour
Provides a morning masterpiece no artist could surrender.

For there is nothing like a new born day in harmony with life,
The movement of a tranquil sea makes contrast with the strife.
The boats, the sounds, the rising hills,
Is a treasure for the soul,
To waken to this wondrous sight
Can make the spirit whole.

THE SWALLOW

The Swallow is born in perfect form
Its flight a wonderful display
With acrobatic deftness it flies throughout the day.

It fears, not much, its journey makes
From North to South it rarely breaks
And flies o'er mountains, seas and lakes
The venerable exploring swallow.

And from its active life we might learn
Through its actions we might follow,
For its life, though short, there are lessons taught
By the remarkable bird, the swallow.

The chick obeys the parents cries
A survival must lest it dies
From Winter's cold before it flies
From England's shores, the swallow.

And in October they are gone
In search of pastures warm,
But on a bright summer day
We shall see that acrobatic display
Once again from that beautiful bird, the swallow.

HEAT ON A SINGAPORE STREET

Air-conditioned office, outside looking grey
Not a true reflection, the heat is here to stay
Rain clouds gather overhead, storms and flashing light
But the temperature stays consistent
Even through the night.

Rainstorms lend some short relief, to the raging sun,
But once the cloud has passed on by
Another scorcher has begun.
All the blocks and sun creams
Can't keep the rays at bay
And still the labourer works on through the ravages of the day.

Oh how I wish for a cool breeze
Or even some quenching sleet!
As I feel the serrated edge of the sun's relentless heat.
The trees that once protected us
And cooled both head and feet
Have long since been removed
And replaced by hot concrete.

People stumble forward
As they pass by friends they meet
For there is no time to chatter
In the heat on a Singapore Street

THE WRITING ON THE WALL

The Writing's on the wall,
But how often do we read it?
The Writing's on the wall,
We never think we'll need it.

Stare into the mortar cracks,
See the imperfections there.
The alignment of each brick,
Each troweled lick,
That shows the builder's flare.

The Writing's on the wall,
And time will overlay it.
So read on fast it will not last,
As the message changes tack,
Through winds of time,
We lose each line,
Read wisely now and heed it.

A WORK IN PROGRESS

Marriage is a work in progress.
As you learn to understand each other
day by day
Until that understanding might transcend and overcome all
such trials sent your way.

Enjoy your own company and share each memory.
Covet this memory as a prized possession.
Always Appreciate, show patience, love, forgive and more,
be content with what you share together.
Complete the circle of your lives like a fortress wall.
This structure built in the mind might soften
any fall and rebuild.
For Marriage is a selfless devotion of respect.
Never more tried or tested than in that one commitment
devoted to pursuing your own very special happiness
together.

FEELINGS OF FEAR

There is nothing to fear except fear itself.
This is very true.
The fear lies in imagination.
It all lies deep inside of you.
Confront that fear which might affect your life; a physical
    blow, a scheming act of callousness which strikes as deep
    as any knife.
Draw a line within yourself to differentiate,
The imposter from reality and that line shall be your gate.

BAD BACK

Why do they call a sore, painful back "Bad?"
I have often wondered why,
Though just cannot figure out no matter how I try.
It's not done a thing that's wrong
Mostly it's been right, but just of late
It's been a pain and kept me up at night!
I remember when I'd arch for fun and try cartwheels as well,
But no longer can I try these things
My back has gone to hell.
I'll take a walk that's in my mind
I shall take to fields and hills,
But before I do I must take a few of those pain relieving pills.
I've stretched, touched toes and exercised
Really done my best, but at the end it's the same result, my
    back won't pass the test.
And there's the answer my back is getting old
While telling me, it's not to make me sad,
But rather that my old back is plain and simply "Bad"

THE BRITISH PUB

Britain was built on beer
It's history in a jar,
The words of wisdom spoken
By laymen around the bar.

The country inn and city hotel
The world that stopped
At the sound of a bell

Sippers and slurpers
Beer fueled the workers,
Making heaven to some,
Out of hell.

A walk in the Dales
Whether snow blows or hails
Would only end up in one place
Where you are welcomed by all,
Picked up if you fall
And given an ear and some space.

DON'T GIVE UP ON EACH OTHER

Let's try to stay together
And not castigate the blame.
We all have input to situations
in our own name.

We need to step back once and hold together twice,
From those situations in our life which don't turn out very nice.
There will always be the trouble maker, the finger pointing blame,
But which one of us can stand up tall and say it was never in
     their name.

We try to dodge each issue, we say it wasn't me,
But we're no longer children with sibling rivalry.
We're adults grown to lead, we set example as our creed,
Not tell tale little people who sit by while others bleed.

I feel that we must bond and heal, give negative press a rest.
Those punters on the TV, we know, are just a well paid pest.
They like the sound of their own voice made with little
     thought or none.
They will still be talking nonsense when the room is an empty one.
So man up, be strong don't take too long to forgive your
     fellow friend.
Who knows, You might even need their strength and
     comfort at some stage in the end.

LEVELLING UP...

We had it all, up here in the North,
The Industry, the jobs, the wealth,
Albeit at the detriment of health.

And now we plead and beg for an equal share
Yet when it was here, what did we care?
Graft was etched into every soul,
From Steel to Mills, docks, cullet and coal.
From the canals to the rails we captured it all,
But blinkered our thinking not set for a fall.

We took it for granted both poor and the rich,
Built estates on masses of land,
Captured public space and added to a prosperous life for the
    grand.
Created a majesty, a life envied by all,
The upwardly destined, not prepared for a fall.

Not prepared, but greedy for more,
Wide eyed envy from an opposite shore.
Earned in the North and spent in the South,
Not much has changed,
It is still all hand to mouth.

SMILING TIGER

Smiling Tiger
Every smile tells a lie
Smiling Tiger
Don't take off your eye.
It smiles like a friend
You'd trust 'till the end.
Smiling Tiger beware
The friendship you share.
Smiling Tiger
Might purr as you ruffle its fur
As it swishes its tail and closes its eyes
Take care and look deeper
This is all a disguise.

KING OR PAUPER

King or pauper the end is the same
Rich or poor the road will be hard
And all that's left is your name.
No values in life if you're dealt the wrong card.
You can't choose destiny,
You can only decide.
The unfolding of life will be clear.
The path, undulating, never straight, never smooth,
No matter what possessions or persona we put on!
The choices we make, the actions we take,
Will live on, long after we are gone.

YES WE REMEMBER

Yes we remember, each year
Yes we remember and maybe shed a tear
Yes for the brave souls that went before
Yes for the children of many a war.
Yes for the mothers and fathers left behind
Yes for their memories which hurt each time
they find.....
A reminder of their loss.....
A poppy, medal, letter or a cross.
Yes we shall remember ...... in silence.

ABSENT MOMENTS

To absent friends we raise our glass
And "absent" was the teacher's word in class
Absent minds which tend to stray
Absent deeds left undone all day.

Who vanished from the scene?
Whose life is like a mystic's dream?
Who is there but seldom seen?
A friend, on whose shoulder we can lean.

Grandad sitting in his chair
Sadly he is no longer there.
His presence felt by those who care
His spirit we all love and share.

In our lives what do we lose
And how much do we find?
How much do we throw away
And what do we leave behind?

Absence makes the heart grow fonder,
We never miss until it is gone.
We lead our lives just for the moment
Which can't rewind as we pass on.

SCRAPPED OR NOT?

I was hired, then got fired
So I retired.
I then got rehired, then got tired
So I retired (before I expired).

Who do these companies think they are?
Using people like an old used car.
Once a gleaming, pristine, classy chassis in a magazine
But then the engine skips a beat
The comfort has gone from the leather seat
Costs increase to keep it on the road
The owner thinks he will just off load!

But there is a twist in this piece of steel
Everyone doesn't view it as old or Jurassic
Rather it has become a collector's classic.
Rebuilt, strong and good as new,
It is back on the road
And if you want it, then join the queue.

OUT TO LUNCH

Out to lunch!
We are so
Not sure which way to go.
Because we have issues on our mind
We are in the city of the blind
And absently we wend our way
Not knowing when to be there or knowing when to stray.
The mobile's ringing, texts to do!
My mind is blinkered,
Life's a zoo!
Head down in wonderment
Of the latest message sent.
Like the ostrich, head in sand
As you listen to the band.
Headphones on crossing roads,
Absent lives which might explode.
We are swept up by our plans
Much higher achievement life demands,
But standards they're just going nowhere
Absent like our mind's not been there!
Now here's a warning do it fast
Absenteeism will not last.
You have to be there, friend, be told
To pave your street of life with gold.

MOTHERS CHILD

There is nothing to replace a Mothers touch and smile,
Her presence which is always there to calm a fearful child,
The one who we depend upon to give us strength within,
The one who will stand by us from the beginning to the end.
And though a Mothers passing will leave her child perplexed,
Her soul, at peace, a Mother will be with us from this world
    to the next.

MISSING MOMENTS

You never miss the water until the well runs dry
And you never miss the summer until the last swallows fly.
You never miss a friend, until those friends die
And the memories are all we have despite the tears we cry.

No we never miss, 'til it's too late, we never miss a thing
While working hard to get things done and for our future
    bring.

DYING TRADITION

Then Grandma passed a silver florin into my hand,
I understand that Grandad commented, "He'll do, he's
    grand"
And Uncle Charlie was the one to wet the baby's head,
Then I would be baptised in church, on time, as planned.

In Greece my son's blond hair was affectionately touched,
    with care.
Followed by the gesture of a spit! Ensuring goodness
    prevailed over 'it'
The 'Evil Eye' which through our lives would come to spy,
To neutralise this pupil of doom, laying it ineffective,
    dormant and bare.

Where does superstition and tradition cross or overtake?
Each celebration marked with a cake,
Or carry the bride, in moral code, to commence the marriage
    on the road.
Traditional sense of fear or celebration or making most of
    each occasion?

But tradition dies as we learn more,
The umbrella opened inside the door.
The Morris dancers take their last stride,
No traditional deeds or words of wisdom given to a youthful
bride.

For equality in all we do has suffocated the old wives tale,
As the running water from the tap, long since removed the
pail,
So the progress of our life prevails and hence it will remain,
With nothing of tradition left, the future shall never be the
same.

A MARRIAGE

Marriage is a journey not a race.
No finish line, just a summary of effort concluded at the
    couple's shared pace.
The road is new on each event,
No signs or guidelines, only the obstacles of life to
    circumvent.

To try and not succeed is common place,
And to fail does not mean a fall from grace,
Nor does success bring a trophy or a prize,
Just another milestone which at the roadside lies.

The years are marked by Silver and Gold
Which are far less precious than the stories told
Of laughter and tears, just part of life,
A true testament of devotion and courage to a Husband and
    Wife.

MY GENERATION

My generation was yesterday
Cloth caps, Top hats and Bowlers,
A transition from gentry to mods, rockers and rock 'n
    rollers,
My generation was all about class,
Working, middle and upper class with pretentious brass.
My generation was flower power, fitters, miners, weavers
    and dockers
All working around the clockers.
Seven days, double time Sundays, three shifts, three hundred
    and sixty five
To keep heads above water and survive.
My generation was a changing one,
From land line to mobile and working on the run.
From own office, own desk, own space,
To own hot desk, own nothing, a real rat race.
My generation built a dream, but created a mess.
My generation might be the start of creating a wilderness.
My generation travelled by bus then transferred to a car.
My generation went through the after math of World War II.
Now my generation is living in a kind of zoo.
Equality for all, the class system gone, everyone searching to
    live in the sun.
Everyone wants a share of the pie, work from home, zero hours,

We are now living in Ivory Towers.
Diesel and petrol may become obsolete,
We may end up walking on the street.
The roads once cared for now a crumbling mess,
Once laughing at life now overtaken by stress.
My generation created standards and broke all the rules,
Who were we kidding when we're governed by fools,
Guessing their way and forecasting what?
Our pace of progress now reduced to a trot.
The next generation needs to awake
Or there shall be no one on which, to blame our mistake.

CHASING RAINBOWS

I used to be Black and White
But hey; now realise I am not.
Like everyone I'm simply Grey.

We need all the spectrum of colours
To make life white
And no colours at all to make life
Dark as night.

No point chasing rainbows.

LESSON FROM AN INFANT

I caught the chill, the overspill of ones egotistic ways.
A lifetime of working, search and energy
Dismissed to my dismay.
My contribution in good faith to help all those around
Undone by one clean cut, of forces underground.
How can we live in Godly ways?
How can these sins prevail?
Are these the values of today?
And do our morals pale?
Against our past upbringing, against a sense of pride,
Today is not as yesterday, when we stood side by side.
Today's value is the bottom line
And all is fair, be told;
Don't hold a view too highly
And youth you must not scold.
Is this the way, the weary way that we've turned out to be?
And will it take an eternal life to return to purity?
For what has the strain of ones self-gain
Put on the stress of life?
The answer I feel is clear to see
And sharp as the sharpest knife.
If we can strive and learn to be of that which we are born,
A humble infant, with no vanity of mind, no greed, all heart,
    no scorn.

AMBITION

Ambition is a good thing
When earned through sacrifice,
But ambitions shouldn't be achieved
Through sacrifice of others
Or any other price.

VALENTINE

Commemorating a time of Valentine,
Love is the joy and pleasure of two when
All treasures of the world are left behind.
A satisfaction that lies in bliss and ignites the soul with a
solitary kiss.

IN CONTRAST

I read about the snows and gales,
The high seas and other stormy weather.
As I sit gazing at tall still trees
And tight knit foliage close together.

I look at the stark grey skies of night,
At the thunderous blackened moon
And wonder, as the shadow hides the light
Which masks me from the heat of noon.

The cold wind pinches at my face
And fingers numb begin to ache.
As warm winds myself embrace
And on the sun drenched sands
I slowly soften and relax in grace.

It's far too cold to venture out,
Unless covered like an Eskimo
And here I sit in shirt and shorts
With nothing but my peaceful thoughts

I'm wet, drenched cold right to the bone,
I need a ride to get me home.
The warm rain runs gently down my back
As I amble slowly across the jungle track.

Cold and frosty chilled the star filled night,
The moon's reflection shining bright.
Dull black the sky and hazy heat, no stars above,
As mosquitoes bite and in doors I do retreat.

GOLFING TYPES

How many types of golfer are there?
Let me name a few
And if you are not in here,
There's room for volume two.

Golfers come and golfers go
Some play fast and some play slow.
There are talkers and sulkers
And those who can't play,
I just wonder why they turn up here each day!

We have boasters and chokers,
Who move sods with great ease,
But never replace, they just do as they please.
There are moaners and groaners
Who blame all but their swing,
They never admit; golf is just not their thing!

There are thrashers and cursers
And those who are worse'rs
They stand around swinging
And look like rehearsers.

There are golfers with etiquette and those without
Who tread on your line and shuffle about,
When you're playing a stroke or eyeing a putt
There's always that golfer who just does your nut.

There are muckers and suckers,
Some have no luckers
Who hit objects that just don't exist!
And pretend looking down at the ill fated club
It had nothing to do with their wrists.

There are carriers and trolley'ers,
Puffers and panters
Who rattle and roll, get out of control,
As they chase looking red in the face,
Their cart over hills which so often spills
And change the course to an obstacle race!

There are dressers and messers and vicars who bless us,
They also forgive all our sins,
As we leave the very last hole (19th) Without any control
Of our speech or the use of our pins.

KILLING TIME

The Day's begun
Get some emails done.
A coffee in the Mall
A chat with some old pal.
A walk, a browse
At hedges, fields of sheep and cows.
A time to read and write,
Let your mind wander.
What are your beliefs?
Let the train of thought meander
Is there a meaning to this rhyme?
Or am I just killing time?

NOTES

NOTES

NOTES

NOTES

www.ingramcontent.com/pod-product-compliance
Lightning Source LLC
Chambersburg PA
CBHW032017040426
42448CB00006B/646